Golden Days

Brenda Eldridge
and
Stephen Matthews

Other titles by Brenda Eldridge

POETRY

The Silver Cord 2009

Facing Cancer 2011

Tangled Roots - new and collected poems
- edited by Jude Aquilina -2014

Wonderment 2015

Connecting 2019

Stepping Into the Blue - 2023

Sounds & Silences 2023

Dancing Dots 2023

Simple Pleasures - 2024

NON-FICTION

From Patagonia to Australia - Collected Prose 2015

Homespun Tapestry 2016

Flower Child 2021

Liminal 2022

Golden Days
Copyright©2026 Brenda Eldridge and Stephen Matthews
Print ISBN: 978-1-76109-732-4
ebook ISBN: 978-1-76109-733-1
Cover design: by Graham Davidson
Cover photo supplied by Brenda Eldridge

First published 2026 by
GINNINDERRA PRESS
PO Box 2 Bentleigh 3204
ginninderrapress.com.au

Contents

Introduction	5
Stephen	6
Brenda – July 2025	7
Debbie – January 2026	8
Not Just Words	11
Crows Don't Lie	12
Waiting Room	13
On Our Raft	14
Yorke Peninsula	15
He Is My Home	18
Stephen's Girls	19
We've Done It Again	20
On Our Own	21
Slowly and Reluctantly	22
Dying Not Dead	23
Precious Time	24
Tunnels of Trees	25
Unexpected Oasis	26
Return of Peace	27
Hint of Autumn	28
Red Spot	29
Bitter-sweet	30
Until World's End	31
Golden Autumn	32
Suspended	33
Treasure	34
Silent Night – Holy Night	35

Golden Days	36
Moonlight and Lilies	37
Remembering to Breathe	38
Daffodils	39
Become the Universe	40
Broken Pieces	41
Written Word	42
Egg Boots and Egg Head	43
Wrong Colours, Wrong Words	44
Heaps and Buckets	45
Blurred Vision	46
Blinding Light	47
Boxes Neatly Ticked	48
A Good Morning	49
Time Passing	50
Guard Dog	51
Not Wishing Time Away	52
Vigil	53
Flames	54
Tenderness	55
Sacred Song	56
Sea Glass	57
Silver Light	58
To the Point of No Return	60

Introduction

It's January 2024, and all our worst fears have become hard reality. This time there will be no life-saving surgery. The doctors, knowing the huge and cumbersome system has failed us, offered palliative care like some panacea. We are not the same as in 2010 when almost ten hours of surgery and six weeks of radiotherapy allowed us precious years. We created a life together of such rich fulfilment, doing what we both did best – writing, editing, publishing and loving. Sadly, it also included heartaches too savage to take in properly, which left us weakened, as we step into this last arena of our lives together.

Not only having to grapple with the bastard cancer, Stephen had to decide the future of Ginninderra Press. As a graduate from Cambridge University in his early twenties, he knew he wanted to publish books. A well-meaning careers advisor discouraged him and directed Stephen into teaching. Years passed, immigration to Australia happened but by the time Stephen was fifty he was in a position to fulfil his dream and started up Ginninderra Press. It is the child of his soul. Ginninderra Press enabled him to change lives, though it is fair to say, he had no real idea of the difference he was making until he published my poetry and took me into his world as his wife and fellow editor.

In 2021, twenty-five years after he began Ginninderra Press, Stephen was awarded the Order of Australia Medal for services to Australian publishing. This was without doubt, the proudest moment of his life. He had a vague plan to slow down when he had either sold 300,000 books or turned eighty. We had talked about who could take over the press and there was never any doubt we would be asking Debbie Lee. How wonderful was her response when this conversation was had much sooner than any of us had imagined. And yes, we did exceed that goal of book sales.

Now we are in our golden days. The bastard cancer is winning the physical war but hasn't come close to damaging who we are and the love we share, the love that will continue.

Stephen

The careers advisor Brenda writes of, who steered me away from trying to enter the publishing world after university, was right to do so, though not, I suspect, for the reasons he thought. I needed the years between graduating and starting Ginninderra Press to acquire the experience, knowledge and skills that enabled me to make the business successful.

Even then, it wasn't easy. Starting an independent publishing house with scant resources is not for the faint-hearted. It was some years before the business made any profits and some years more before those profits became significant. The turning point was when Debbie Lee, who had known me when I managed the Co-op Bookshop at the Australian National University in the 1990s, got in touch with me to see if I would be interested in publishing through Ingram Spark. Debbie had recently joined Ingram Spark, who offer print-on-demand services and worldwide distribution. A little research confirmed that, to me, Ginninderra Press and Ingram Spark would be an ideal fit. Suddenly, our books were available worldwide, many of them in ebook editions as well as print. Sales blossomed.

As time went on after doctors treated my oral cancer in

2010, we more or less forgot the drama of the surgery, and the subsequent radiotherapy and recuperation, reminded only by yearly check-ups. When, after a year of growing symptoms, it was confirmed that the cancer had returned (or a new one had emerged), and I was told I had up to six months to live, we entered a period of deep shock. Brenda turned of course to writing poetry, which has sustained her through previous crises. I entered a period of reflection on my life and the things that have been important to me. In my reflection, I have been sustained by the love of family and friends. Brenda has carefully collected the emails and cards that have come in from far and wide. So far, I haven't been able to read more than a few of them, knowing that the love and kindness will be overwhelming.

Ginninderra Press was my pride and joy for nearly twenty-eight years and I'm glad Brenda shared and enriched the last half of that time. The poems in *Golden Days* give a vivid picture of why our time together has been so extraordinarily fulfilling. Golden Days indeed.

Brenda – July 2025

After in-depth discussions and with the help of the Voluntary Assisted Dying pathway, Stephen took his last breath on 25 September, 2024. We had longer than the doctors indicated. It wasn't long enough – it could never have been long enough.

We did what we agreed to do, faced whatever happened with dignity and grace. I did what he asked. I kept our daily lives throughout as normal as possible. He left reclining in his big chair in the cosy corner where we spent so many blissful hours. We were listening to Dolly Parton and Kris Kristofferson singing 'Love

You to the Moon and Back' not the exquisite strains of Richard Strauss 'Four Last Songs' as some people would have expected knowing Stephen (we did have this playing in the gentle peace earlier). Again, adhering to his express wishes, Stephen had a direct cremation, there was no funeral service, no gathering of family and friends to share stories and warm love. His ashes are spread beneath the tree his daughter gave us years ago in the garden he loved so much. He was waiting for the tree to be big enough to sit under – this was as close as we could get.

Stephen was a modest man of incredible vision and unbreakable determination. He did what others dream about or talk about. He was always alert for authentic voices. These voices became his voice in our community. None of us will ever know just how far the influence of those voices has been felt. Those of us writers who have been blessed to be in the Ginninderra Press family will ever be grateful to Stephen Matthews.

I wrote a lot of poetry in our last months together. *Golden Days* is a little peek into our world…a world that now only lives in memory as hard reality insisted I not only lose my beloved husband, but that I must move out of the home we shared beside the tidal reach for almost sixteen years.

Debbie – January 2026

11 a.m. 25 September 2025. Brenda and I are chatting to two young women at the Collins Bookshop counter, Mount Gambier. Brenda looks up at the clock and lets out a gasp. It is exactly one year to the minute that Stephen had taken his medication – and then, his last breath.

We two *older* women were on our much-vaunted 'Thelma and Louise' trip, to mark the anniversary of Stephen's passing and to honour his life. So busy talking up Ginninderra Press, we almost missed the moment. I imagine Stephen, always so unassuming yet quietly self-assured, chuckling softly at our antics.

Books are after all, his gift to the world and his greatest wish was that his legacy lives on. It is an honour beyond compare to be carrying Ginninderra Press forward and upholding Stephen's vision – but as Brenda insists, with my own stamp.

I met Stephen during my first job as a publishing sales rep. I turned up on the doorstop of the ANU Uni Coop in tears, having just crashed my new company car. I think I made an impression! Reconnecting many years (and jobs) later, it was like time had stood still. Only by now, Stephen had relocated to Adelaide, and he had Brenda by his side. Having introduced him to 'print-on-demand', our working lives became intertwined and Stephen invited me to launch *Rays of Light: Ginninderra Press – the first 20 years*, (collated by his and Brenda's great friend, Joan Fenney).

It is hard to believe that was 10 years ago. Many trips to Adelaide later and nights spent chatting with a cup of tea or perhaps a glass of wine, and here we are, without Stephen but still with Ginninderra Press, a 30-year milestone. Brenda and I remain steadfast, and the privilege of publishing *Golden Days,* this lyrical, grief-struck, love-filled ode to Stephen is profound.

Not Just Words

Every night for years
Before we slept
Stephen touched my feet with his
Every night my response was the same:

Goodnight Mr Foots
And the amazingly adoring
Constant steadfast
Loyal loving
Discerning
Splendidly devoted
Thrillingly manly
Exuberant enthusiastic
Intrepid indomitable
Irrepressible irresistible
Inexhaustible
But gently weddedly
Intrusive heels and toes

My guys

Crows Don't Lie

One for sorrow
Two for joy

One landed in the big pine
While we were eating breakfast
It craaked loudly to make certain
I knew it was there
And flew away

The same crow or his mate
Came back two days later
Same time same place same actions

I knew what the message meant –
Affirmation of what was coming
What was already here

I listened to the doctors words and thought
Crows don't lie

Waiting Room

No pressures
This precarious time
No questions
No answers we want to hear
Except it's all a horrible mistake

A different way of measuring time
Army time – hurry up and wait –
Doesn't really apply

Can't say it's huge faceless and uncaring –
Is this one of those waiting for god times?

All ages and backgrounds congregate here
I don't make eye contact
Perhaps if I do I will get lost
In too much knowledge

I don't seem to want or need anything
It's a strange nothingness
Not knowing how to put my next foot down

On Our Raft

The surgeon shocked us to the core
Filled us with terror
And then flung us out to sea

We sit precariously balanced on our raft
Afloat on a vast ocean
With wind and waves sending us where they will
(No one has any answers)
We don't know if this present course of radiation
Is going to make any difference

Are we being shuffled from pillar to post
So someone can say
We ticked all the boxes
Did everything possible
But they do not – cannot tell us about time

We do not have the comfort of a safe place to land
Only this vast ocean of life

Yorke Peninsula

Hurriedly, Stephen's daughter, her son and daughter, flew from the other side of the world to spend precious time with him. We rented a holiday-let in Point Turton, SA for two nights and meandered around part of the Yorke Peninsula making memories…

        Tiny white butterflies
        Turn into fishing craft
        Skimming home to port
        Across a blue tablecloth

        Ocean seeps gently to shore
        Barely a ripple
        As it covers rocks
        That lie shallow on the sand

        Flash of light
        Sun on a passing dolphin
        A spark ignited

        Gum blossoms
        Glittering leaves
        Move like ballroom dancers
        In a gentle breeze

        Safe harbour beckons
        Small craft make haste
        As if running before a storm

        Stillness silence
        All embracing
        A tangible presence

Tree silvered and twisted
By sun wind age
Perfectly balanced

Two white butterflies
In perfect harmony
Flit across a garden
In a world of their own

Sickle moon
Watches
Her power
Moving the sea

Looking towards the lowering sun
I saw a huge pelican fishing for supper
Before he stood tall in the water
And took off

Sleepy birds
Sunset gossipping
Soft bark hanging
Swinging like
Washing on a line

Thundering white foam
Many-blued sea
Pristine golden sand
Wind to blow away
Cobwebs and send
Spindrift filled with rainbows
Flying high

Long long roads
Arrow straight
Rising falling
Reminder of how
Big this land is
No need for bends
Just a line in the dirt
From one place to another

Ducks swimming past
Too many to count
Like homing pigeons
Unerringly they go –
We all need a home

In the vast ocean of life
We all long for home
A safe harbour of respite
Before we must set sail again

Into a warm evening
A fresh breeze
Taking a stinging sun
Down and away
Drawing a good day
To a close
Easing senses to quiet

Long shadows
Now soothing
Ending a day
Of sunshine and sea

He Is My Home

In silent darkness
Beside my sleeping man
I can at last put words
To my deepest grief

When he dies
I will lose my home

Perhaps his steady breathing
Will still be heard
In the velvet softness of night

Perhaps I will still hear his voice
Saying 'chill' when I get upset

Maybe if I listen carefully
I will become the still core
In the cyclone of every day life
As he has been for me

Stephen's Girls

Soon Stephen's daughter, his two granddaughters and I
Will come together to have linked tattoos
Daffodil is his birth month flower

My daffodil is joined with a marigold
I will have an S and B entwined
Among the stems
And a small red ladybird
As a symbol of home

His daughter will have Dad entwined in hers

I wonder what the young women will choose…

We've Done It Again

It only took four daily visits
To be recognised at the radiotherapy clinic
My tattoo has drawn admiring comments
Especially when I tell the story behind mine
And the ones the girls now wear

Our quiet questions have been answered
My moments of angst calmed
Showing our appreciation to the nursing staff

It doesn't take much to be polite and pleasant
And it does make such a difference
To the lives of those in difficult circumstances

On Our Own

On our own there is little angst
We go at our own pace
Keeping appointments
Making pleasant conversation in passing
There is a steadiness now
Shock recognised and eased
Our needs simplified

Slowly and Reluctantly

I sat on his lap and wept
He asked why and I said
'You are poorly and I can do nothing'

He pondered briefly and said
'I am not poorly
I am dying
Slowly and reluctantly
But I am dying'

Dying Not Dead

My son taught me about dead
There was no negotiating with it
No trade-offs
No bargains to be struck
He was dead
He was gone
And all we had to do
Was grieve and learn
And we have done this

I waited for my parents and the father
Of my children to die
They were long and troubling years
But I didn't contemplate
What my world would be like without them
Because by then
They were no longer an active part of my daily life

This time I am learning every day about dying

He wakes and says 'I am still here'
And I reply 'then we will have another day'
And we walk through this gift of a day
Doing the ordinary things
That make our life extraordinary
And I try not to think
This might be the last time…
I try and savour the precious moments
Even able to make light of it all
But I still feel I am walking down a dark tunnel
And there seems to be no light at the end for me

Precious Time

Everyone around us has a gift of a day
How many are aware of how precious this time is
So busy doing the day
I hear my old friend W.H. Davies
'What is this life if full of care
We have no time to stand and stare'*

If a busy person came with us
Could they sit calmly
Waiting for things to happen
Or would they be chafing to move on
To do the next thing
Would they try and fill the silence
With empty chatter rather than
Face uncomfortable thoughts
Do they stay away to protect
Or respect our privacy
Or to keep seperate from a reality
Too hard to embrace

* From the poem 'Leisure'

Tunnels of Trees

Leaves of fresh green
Belied that it was late summer
Silver bark twisted like skeins of wool
Gleamed with sunlight
More ghostly than I have ever noticed before
Polished by some invisible hand
To a lustre that ached my heart

What more could I ask for
Than these shared moments
There could never be enough
Yet I hunger not
Here there is patience
An unending stillness
That affirms all is as it must be
There can be nothing else
But appreciation of life's gifts

Unexpected Oasis

The treatment area has its own calm
An oasis from noise and frenetic emotions
Here the staff are always kind and caring
Not false cheer – a reassuring steadiness

We are treated as people
With courtesy and respect
Not just numbers pushed through
On a production line

Return of Peace

We created a haven for ourselves
Some have entered and recognised sacred peace
Others have availed of our hospitality
But brought energy and disruption
And I wonder if they ever knew
The place they were in
The gift we shared

Some people only live in their own space
Taking the sameness with them everywhere
Unable to be open to a different way of being

When they leave the air vibrates for a while
Then birds settle in the garden
Enjoying our usual routines
Bringing their joy of life

We are eased by simple pleasures
Music that warms our souls
Comfortable silences which are the core of us
No angst
No explanations
Mutual nourishment

Hint of Autumn

There is a hint of autumn
In this early morning coolth*
Leaves dance in a passing breeze
That caresses my face
Like a lover's touch

Council extravagant watering
Has gifted emerald grass
To soften summer's dryness
A neighbour's ivy straggles along the fence
Our rosemary bush a mass of flowers
And sleepy bees

The gentle knock of oars
As a rowing four go past on the tidal reach
Intrusive calls of their coxswain

Bob the wattlebird
Pigeons and mynahs
Come into our garden in search of food
And overhead a waning moon
An ever changing constant

* coolth – When I asked Stephen if I could have the word coolth, he said, 'You poets are always creating new words and yes you can have coolth.'

Red Spot

Fifteen years ago he bought me
A small round red rug –
It was where I could stamp my feet
And cry 'It isn't fair'

Under his soothing ways
The raging emotions have dissipated

This morning I came out of the studio
Noticed the red rug had faded from sunlight
And I realised it had been years
Since I felt the need to stamp my feet

Did he break the savage beast –
Did he become lion-tamer extraordinaire?

No
He taught me fighting hurt me most of all
Changed nothing that could not be changed
Emotions from the past that robbed me
Of vital energy I need to make every day
A good day
Nothing has been broken
I have been healed

Bitter-sweet

Words I haven't used – yet on hearing them
Find suit us well
We savour these mornings
Knowing we are in a bubble
Inside a fog with no safe parameters

Even terror has become acceptance
No energy to squander
On ranting and raging

We navigate traffic
On roads bringing him to radiotherapy treatment
Today thirteen of twenty

Until World's End

These precious days
Made up of stolen moments
Hiding them from death

We walk quietly
Hoping we won't be noticed
Talk softly
Laugh gently
Letting tranquility find a home
Within us

Conversation with others is hard
Always unanswerable questions

I heard a crow earlier
Acknowledged I don't forget his message
I saw a ghost egret
I must look up what he had to say
But really it is all the same
Go quietly through the days
Until world's end

Golden Autumn

No one can tell us anything
No certainty one way or the other
Not cast adrift exactly
But the sense of security
Coming in almost every day for a month
Will be gone when we leave today
Armed with creams and dressings
Phone number to contact if we get in trouble
Which of course we will…
This was only delaying tactics
And I am thankful for the extra days

Golden autumn a better way to remember –
I've had enough of harsh reality
Though it has its own beauty
The reality of dramatic clouds
As another day woke up
Changing from dark grey highlighted by vivid pink
As quickly turning to gleaming golden yellow
And this too turning into white –
Sun unmoved by this colour display
Insisting on dominating a pale sky
Where he will ride the day through
Until setting drama takes over
A brief hurrah before night
Another blessed day gone
Never to be experienced again
So many golden days
I could do the arithmetic
But they would be no less precious

Suspended

For a few moments I hung suspended
Like an autumn leaf or stray blossom
Caught on a strand of cobweb across a path

A full moon pale ethereal
Lowered inevitably in the west
While a golden blazing sun
Rose in an apricot sky
Over the eastern hills

Treasure

Early autumn sunlight
Is pouring through our windows
A touch of warmth on my neck

A lute is playing
Timeless notes dancing
Like leaf shadows on the couch

Stephen is doing what he has done
For fifteen years
In the kitchen preparing an evening meal

Except tonight as all days now
It is dinner for one
And I will feed him nutrients via a tube

No amount of gentleness
Not our depths of mutual love
Can change this cruel reality
As we treasure these golden hours

Silent Night – Holy Night

Not the carol associated with Christmas
My silent night – holy night
Happened in the early hours
When my corner of the world was at peace

Can silence call us from sleep?
I believe so

I lay in bed for a while listening
To Stephen breathing and knew relief
Noticed the moonlight
Shining bright beneath the curtains
Left this comfort and walked
Into my studio in the next room

Outside the tidal reach was
A magical pattern of black and silver
With orange lozenges
A dolphin unseen except for
Smooth luxurious ripples
Made everything rock gently
As soothing as any mother's arms

This was a deep silent night
Made holy by my awe of nature
The source of healing

Golden Days

My heart whispers 'Go now
In the glorious splendour of these golden days
Please don't wait for the greyness of winter'

We sit under the veranda on Easter Sunday
Not that it has any special significance for us
And soak up the tranquility of our garden
Everything looks lush and green

A pot of portulaca with their dainty blooms
Shining yellow and deep pink
Another pot of something whose name I have forgotten
A mass of yellow and orange blooms like little trumpets
A new tree – birthday candles
With four banksia flowers yellow with a halo of red
At the far end of the garden a butterfly plant
Has sent up a long stem which leans under its own weight
It nods in a shaft of sunlight
Just like its namesake against the dark shadows
Of the carport beyond

Bob the wattlebird is croaking to a mate
While their youngster sips from the birdbath
A pair of honeyeaters flit across from one tree to another
Pigeons and mynahs still vie for seed

Date palms next door tower over us
Their fronds moving gently in a breeze
Sparkling as if wet from longed for rain

Was there ever a better time to go
If leave he must

Moonlight and Lilies

Silent darkness called me from sleep
I slipped out of bed into the spare room
As I gazed at a golden sickle moon
To offer my prayers of thanks
I could smell the lilies
Their sweet perfume from downstairs
Filled the house
As if they too worshipped the moon

Remembering to Breathe

Dolphin reminds me to breathe
As my mind seeks Earth Mother among native trees
To feel linked again to the child within
Who was at home among trees and flowers

Years ago in the Blue Mountains
There was a glass-bottomed gondola
That traversed from one ridge to another
Far far below treetops bloomed
Like giant green umbrellas

I dared myself to look down
Paralysing terror held me momentarily
Then I grinned
Glad I had been brave enough

I feel like that now
Suspended in a fragile craft
Hovering over the abyss
Trying to remember to breathe
Reminding myself I still can
Because in a heartbeat
Stephen won't be able to
But I will be across
And back on solid ground

Daffodils

My son died when wild daffodils were
In flower just outside the old farmhouse garden
Mother called them Mark's daffodils
They had been growing there for years
From stray bulbs and multiplying
With each passing season
It was so easy to picture them
Pure gold dancing in a breeze
Such joyfulness
I like to believe they eased her aching heart
Feeling loss twofold –
For her daughter and her grandson

Daffodil is the birth flower of my Stephen
As the bastard cancer stalks our days
I wear a new tattoo on my arm
In the hope it will keep me brave
In the unimaginable time ahead

Yesterday I made a decision
I will grow daffodils in the spring
Fill the hexagonal raised bed
With bulbs and watch their green spikes
Push up into the light
Think of these two beloved men
Their hearts as golden as the flowers
And strive to stand as straight and tall
As they both did

Become the Universe

Long long ago on a stormy day
I stood in a tumbling ocean
Glanced up into a wall of water
And was eye to eye with a dolphin

Time ceased its moving

Even now I can recall that moment
With such clarity

The depths I see in Stephen's eyes
Are becoming more and more
Like the dolphin's

How hard will it be for him
To take that final step
And become the universe

Broken Pieces

It is said
Love is enough
And from painful experience
I have disputed this
I say
Alone love is not enough
It must be supported
By loving action

Now when Stephen – best of my loves
Is on the verge of leaving
I said to him
'Your love for me
Is the glue
Which holds the broken pieces
Of Brenda together
Keeping her whole'

Small wonder then
I don't want him to go

Written Word

Stephen the man renowned
For his knowledge and use of words
Was robbed of the power of speech
By the bastard cancer

One day he wrote me a note
His words are now inked on my arm
A constant reminder:
You have enabled me to be me –
To believe in myself and trust myself

And for all our time together
I knew he was doing this for me
I had no idea we were mirroring ourselves

Egg Boots and Egg Head

Clever-clogs predictive text
Changed Ugg boots to Egg boots
Causing a distant imagination
To briefly run riot with welcome mirth

Concentrating on the question
Rather than my surroundings
I hit my head on the closed glass door
Expecting it to be open

I don't only have egg on my face
But an egg-lump on my forehead

What is it with eggs?
Should I be rushing off
To research symbolism of them
Or maybe I just need to slow down
Admit to being as tired as I am
Sit in the cosy corner
Close my eyes and drift
And pray the gods
Will keep watch for a while
As I rest my aching head

Wrong Colours, Wrong Words

Like a pallet
Made up of the wrong colours
There are no words
To express how I feel

I just feel the loss of them

Words – what we shaped lives with –
Our own and other writers
But there are no words
Just this dreadful agony
That finds some release in tears

Heaps and Buckets

'I love you heaps'
'I love you buckets'
'That's all right then
I'll put my heaps
In your buckets'

Countless times we say these words

We bought a shiny metal bucket
I transformed it with paint
To becoming what looked like
A rusty old bucket
Which is now lying partly hidden
Among bark and autumn leaves
At its gaping mouth
A purple flowering heartsease
As if spilling out and onto the garden

Blurred Vision

White-cheeked honeyeater
Dared itself to play in the birdbath
Knowing I was sitting here nearby
He flies up into the tree
Then comes down again
He has a voice like flowing honey
And my vision is blurred
By rainbow-filled tears
As I try to capture
These golden days to keep forever

Blinding Light

From a pearly sky
Early morning winter sun
Blazes hard cold white
Reflected on still waters
Beside a disused lighthouse

Blinding light
Casting long dreamy shadows
Gleaming off old railway tracks
Left as a reminder of a dock once
Bustling with the business of life
Now guiding me along
So I don't go too close to the edge
Fall into water I am not sure
How hard I will swim to be free

Boxes Neatly Ticked

A need to go outside
Feel freshness on my face
I potter in our garden trimming twiggy bits
From native bushes struggling with lack of rain
I moved flowerpots – hid them in a corner
Thinking to throw them out when it's time to move
Then in the dark of night my heart rebelled – said 'No'
We will go to a garden centre and buy pansies of all colours
I will have a riot of flamboyance
Those heartsease blooms will do just that
In their battered old pots

But first we wait for the medical people
A round-table discussion – because our dining table is round
There will be no equality of opinion
We will retain our dignity
They will find ways to not say
'You are no longer economically viable
You have out-lived the allotted time we gave you'

We have become an affront to statistics
All we want is to live
They wish otherwise so they can move on
All boxes neatly ticked

A Good Morning

Midnight wandering when all was still and quiet –
Outside a large waning moon
Glowed hazy orange among clouds
Which would bring long-awaited rain by morning
Blissful bouncing-in-and-out-of-birdbaths rain

I checked the newly planted pansies –
They were nodding contentedly –
I hug myself in secret delight for
Deep in one of the old flowerpots
I found a forgotten bluebell bulb with a new shoot
And hope it did not mind too much being disturbed
And will continue to thrust upwards towards the light
I've moved shade-loving plants from the veranda
Out into the rain

I watch the silver-grey tidal reach
Only a little darker than clouds above
The solitary splash of bright colour on this side of the house
Is a vase of yellow chrysanthemums
On a small table by the window
With Enya singing this is a good morning

Time Passing

Stephen feels the cold so much these days
He doesn't sit out here like he used to
Though he still watches the birds eagerly
Through the windows

Seeing a sickle moon
Made me weep in relief
Another impossible month has gone by
And we are still here

Guard Dog

I happened to walk past your office just now…
You were sitting so still at your computer
I wondered if you had indeed slipped away
Then the persistent cough barked
I felt it was a guard dog warning me
'Keep your distance – he's mine'

But he's not – he is still mine for another hour
Or another day – who knows
He stays here for me
How do I make that count for more
Than my selfish pleasure and need?

Not Wishing Time Away

Leaves barely dance in a breeze
But wind chimes whisper a note or two
Soft and mellow
Timeless in this day of sunshine
A promise of spring

I do not wish time away
These precious days together
Filled with joyful memories –
A walk this morning
Pausing to rest beside the tidal reach

I do not think about the future
We haven't finished this life yet
You won't take the sun with you
You are already in the light
That makes the stars twinkle
And one day – who knows –
We may meet again in the sun

Vigil

Tiny raft named YOUNME
Afloat on a vast ocean
The Sea of Life
Days languishing in the doldrums
Rocked by stormy waves
That threaten to capsize us
Then more precariously calm days

We have been awed
By colourful sunrises and sunsets
Mesmerised as a new moon
Waxes peaks wanes
And yet another new moon appears
Each cycle we know could be our last together

No comfort drawn from a River of Stars
Not for us dead friends and relatives watching over us
We feel we are alone in a huge universe
Which might just be one of many

From all directions comes
A steady flow of warmth
Love held in hearts
Sent to us on the wings of prayers
Love that sustains us
During our lonely vigil

Flames

My flame does not even flicker or waiver
It burns strong low steady
Lighting the way into the unknown
Reminders of faith come unbidden
When I need them most
Not in the dark hours of night
But the bright sun-filled cold days
When life feels relentless

Tenderness

So precious are these days
Filled with calm quiet
No need for conversation
Words aren't important any longer
They require thought a topic interest
Time passes regardless of our awareness
How many last goodbyes can we say
They stop having meaning after a while
But I am painfully mindful
Each night when I kiss you goodnight
Bid you sleep well
Wish you sweet dreams
That this might be the last time
And I am awash with agonised tenderness

Sacred Song

Movement ceasing
Breath slowing
A deepening stillness within

Heart steadily beating
Blood pulsing through veins
Life's sacred song

Silence settling like dust motes
Hovering in the air
Lit by sunbeams

Sea Glass

Fearfully I hold green sea glass in my hand
Aware of distances it has travelled
Picked up with care from familiar beaches
Of a lifetime and half a world away

I hear the pure call of gulls keening
My heart aches with longing
The pull of lost childhood

Now I wrap wisdom and experience
Around me like a tattered shawl
Snapping in the strong winds of life or fate

Shards of pottery
The sharp pain of willow pattern
As memories tumble out of a cupboard
Whose doors I thought safely locked

I would go back in a heartbeat
But there is no one there
And memories don't belong to geography
So I will treasure this gift of green sea glass
And rejoice that I have been remembered

Silver Light

Death has been hovering
Like the sword of Damocles
For months we have walked
The nightmare corridors
Haunted by the bastard cancer
We have been grieving for what we are losing
Even as we continued
To make the best of every day
We have not wasted a moment
Though some have been filled with
Anger terror frustration sorrow

Now death is a certainty
Coming at our invitation in the next few days
Perhaps that is why my heart leaped
With joy and wonder to see a half-moon
Bathing my studio with silver light
Knowing I have few nights left
To listen to him breathing
Not wanting to miss this time
There will be time enough to sleep

His spirit is already part of the light
His face shines like a young lad when wreathed in laughter
His face looks bewildered by what is happening to him
And it is his beloved face the bastard cancer is eating away
Months since it has been free of dressings to hide the wound
For wounded is what he is just like any embattled soldier
A true warrior
Brave courageous honourable stoic
Most of all noble
How could he be anything else but silver light…
Though I tease him about becoming a butterfly

I want so much for him to be free

To the Point of No Return

You asked me to keep things normal
And day after day I did this
As our normal changed almost beyond recognition
No more tasty meals
No more delighting in wine and whiskey
Conversations dwindling to
'Write it down on the boogie board'
Daily visits by nurses for wound care
Daily walks becoming shorter and shorter
The bliss of a few days with a wheelchair
Such freedom was ours
Seeing the anguish in your eyes…
Voluntary Assisted Dying pathway
The correct decision
Barbaric in hints and promises that could not be met
But I brought you
To the point of no return
I did that for you and for me
We chose to do it for us

Stephen Matthews and Brenda Eldridge

www.ingramcontent.com/pod-product-compliance
Lightning Source LLC
Chambersburg PA
CBHW070035040426
42333CB00040B/1679